THE GOOD SIDE OF CHRISTIAN SCIENCE
BY CHRISTIAN D. LARSON
ORIGINALLY PUBLISHED IN 1916

This book edition was created and published by Mamba Press
©MambaPress. Print in 2024

The Good Side of Christian Science

IN taking up this subject, a subject that is attracting world-wide attention at the present time, I wish to say that I have the greatest regard and the highest admiration for the Christian Science movement as a movement, and for the principles upon which the movement is based; and the principal cause of my regard and admiration is this, that I admire everybody and everything that has a great purpose in view, and that works for it with all the power that life can give.

This is something that we all feel and, therefore, whenever we meet an individual with a lofty ideal, someone who knows what he wants, and works for it and lives for it under all sorts of circumstances, we cannot help admiring that individual. We may not always agree with him in every respect; and under certain circumstances it may be unwise to try to agree with him; still, we are bound to admire him to the very highest degree, even though he may not take as broad a view of some things as we would like.

It is the same with institutions and movements. If they have a great object, a great purpose, and a lofty goal, and not only live for their convictions, but actually make good in practical life, we are bound to admire them; especially where we realize that they are inspired with the highest form of sincerity.

In all departments of life it is the weaklings that we sometimes lose patience with, although we ought to be patient with everybody, knowing that it is difficult to find anyone who is not doing his best under the circumstances; still, where we find individuals or institutions that have no purpose in view and that are vacillating and uncertain in connection with everything that has real value in life, we cannot bestow upon them any great degree of admiration; in fact, we are liable to think of them as obstacles to the welfare of the world. This they may be in a sense; nevertheless, they need our sympathy instead of our criticism; but when we meet people who live for something — or institutions that work for something definite — something of extraordinary importance to human welfare, and actually make good in their purpose, we invariably give them our admiration; and in this age this spirit of admiration for the successful, for the true, for the sincere and the genuine is growing rapidly; and there is a psychological reason for this fact — something that we shall find it important to respect and admire if we have greater success or higher attainment in view.

In this connection we should remember that we never find successful people among those who are constantly criticising or antagonizing, or who live in the spirit of destruction. The reason is, those people are not living or working in that vital current of life that is moving toward greater things. They are at war with themselves because at war with others; and no mind that is living in continual warfare can ever develop or produce anything of great worth in the world. We cannot afford, therefore, to live in the critical spirit under any circumstances; but when we enter the opposite spirit, that is, when we begin to admire and respect both individuals and institutions that are moving forward, that are successful, that are working for great things — it is then that we get into the great constructive current of life and begin to move with that current into the larger, the higher, the finer and the richer in all the domains of existence.

The best advice that we could give to any young man or woman would be this: "Look at those who have succeeded greatly and achieved largely; then find their secret and apply it in your own life, or improve upon it if you can; but pay no attention to the weakness of those who have failed or lost, because it is the ways of success and not the ways of failure that should be imitated or selected as ideals?'

If all young men would take this advice they would place their minds in a strong, constructive current; and this current would gradually gain force and power so that in the course of time their mental capacity would be increased to a very large degree. In consequence, they would not only enter the pathway that invariably leads to success, but they would constantly increase all those elements of mind and talent that make for still greater success.

The spirit of the age is entering more and more into the understanding of this idea; that is, that the human mind, to be true to itself, must follow constructive lines invariably; and therefore we are learning to apply this idea more and more, not only to individuals, but to institutions and world movements, including religious movements, and all systems of thought in this same manner. We are beginning to overlook as far as possible their weak points and are beginning to give more and more credit to the good and the helpful elements that they all do surely contain. We know that all individuals and all institutions have weak points, but our purpose must be to search for their strong points, and then apply those strong points to ourselves, and improve upon them as far as we possibly can.

This is the spirit of the present age; and it is in this spirit that we will consider the Christian Science movement with a view of finding the reason why that movement has been so very successful along certain lines of action, and why it has accomplished so much regardless of obstacles and persecutions.

There is a strong tendency among a large number of people to criticise new religious institutions, because they say we have too many religions already. Their idea is that we should not formulate any new religious system, but rather aim to unite all religious systems into one; but here we should remember that the ideal of religious union, that is, combining all the churches into one institution, is a dream that will not be realized at present, nor would we want it to be realized for many a long day.

There are in the world something like two hundred different types of mentality in the present age, and each type needs a different form of worship and belief; that is, each type needs a method of its own for approaching the Absolute, or reaching up toward the higher and finer life; and therefore we need all these different systems so that these many types of mind may have modes of aspiration and worship that will suit their present state of development. In another century there may not be so many types of mind, because the farther the human race develops the closer we all come together in understanding and consciousness; but so long as all these many types do exist we need corresponding systems of belief, of worship, of study, of living.

We must not find fault, therefore, with the fact that there are so many religions in the world. They are all necessary just now. If we were to find fault at all it would be this, that most of those religions do not, to use an ordinary term, "make good" in their own field. In brief, they are not living up to their highest light, or trying to make the best use of the gifts and possibilities in their possession.

When we learn to take a broad and reasonable view of all things, we come to the conclusion that no system of thought or no organization should disappear so long as it has a mission, or so long as there is a field wherein it can find useful work; but we do demand that every church, every system of thought, every philosophy, every science, every form of worship make good in the field where it may find its mission at the present time. We cannot commend any institution that is only half alive, or that is wasting the larger part of its opportunity. Such institutions have no right to exist; but an institution that is true to its purpose, true to its mission, and that is turning on the full current, so to speak, of all its power, to the end that it may render the greatest service possible to those with whom it may be concerned — such an institution is absolutely necessary for the time being and cannot fail to win the highest respect of all men and women who have the greatest welfare of the human race at heart.

The fact is, however, that there are very few systems of thought, or religious institutions of the present day, that are really making good in their own field. Many of them are doing fairly well, but there are only a few that are really making full and effective application of the principles upon which they stand.

One of these exceptional few is the Christian Science Church. As an institution this church is certainly making full and effective application of its own principles; and therefore we cannot hesitate to express our greatest admiration and our highest regard once more. It is indeed more than can be said of most of the other religious institutions in the world today; and the fact that the Christian Science Church is making full and effective application of its principles is one reason why it is so successful; but there are many other reasons, and we wish to consider all these reasons carefully so that we may apply them in our own individual life, in our business, in our education, or in any field of religious study that we may undertake now or in the future.

However, before we proceed to examine the inner secret, so to speak, of the Christian Science movement, we should remember that this movement is not for everybody; but the same is true of trigonometry, of agriculture, of chemistry, of domestic science. They are not for everybody. They are for those who need them. The same is true of a great many things, and, in fact, of nearly all things. Every particular system or factor may fill a special place and supply the need of a certain type of mind; and so long as that particular movement, institution or factor does supply the need of a certain type of mind, we should be glad that it is here, and not under any circumstances find fault.

The Christian Science movement occupies a most important mission. It is doing a marvelous work for a certain type of mind; but it is suited only to that certain type, and therefore must not be looked upon as the last word in religion, in science or in truth. It has, like all other institutions, arisen for the purpose of supplying a certain need for the time being; but no institution in itself is permanent. All institutions are destined to give place to other institutions that will arise to supply the new needs of advancing humanity; but for the present age, and possibly for many centuries, the Christian Science movement will continue as a wonderful power for good in the lives of those thousands and thousands who may need that service that Christian Science alone can render.

When we proceed to examine the Christian Science movement we should remember at the outset that whenever we consider a plant, or anything that has developed, we must not only consider the plant itself, but also the seed, and the soil, and the tiller of the soil. In considering this movement, therefore, we must consider, not simply the movement alone, but where and how it came into being; why it grew; and we should also consider the psychological side, because it is the psychological side that holds the secret everywhere.

When we turn our attention to the middle of the past century we find that the human mind was at that time in a peculiar condition, the cause of which may be found by going back to the early part of that century. In examining the mode of thought as it existed in the early part of the past century we find that a number of liberal movements were beginning to take shape and form, and that considerable unrest among a great many people was becoming evident where previously perfect satisfaction obtained with things as they were.

There was considerable preaching against the old order; and a great many minds, some of them spiritual and mental giants, arose in that day to champion mental liberty, arousing thereby a strong sentiment in favor of freedom from the creeds of the day and the awful dogmas that the race had inherited from the past. This commotion in the world of thought in this country continued until about the middle of the century, when some strange things happened — the appearance of various forms of mystical phenomena which literally shook the earth.

The appearance of these phenomena, largely physical in their nature, aroused more curiosity among those who had become dissatisfied with the old order; and people began to think and wonder more and more about the great question, "What is truth?" Thousands and tens of thousands became interested in the various psychical manifestations that appeared at the time, and that continued to mystify the human mind more and more up until the end of the century; and the question was everywhere if these phenomena did contain real truth, because if they did it

THE GOOD SIDE OF CHRISTIAN SCIENCE 7

was evident that the old order was composed of a huge bundle of mistakes. No definite conclusions, however, were formulated at the time; but all this study and research and investigation certainly did prepare the minds of thousands of people for something else, something that would satisfy where the old order had largely failed.

The various liberal movements that were active at the time satisfied a few people, but those movements were more intellectual than otherwise, and therefore were limited in their power to serve the needs of that vast host that was coming out from the old system of belief. The mystical movement that arose at the time with its strange phenomena created much curiosity and much thought, but somehow did not satisfy the yearnings of the soul. This movement did not bring a science, or a philosophy, or a religion that really touched the inner or higher side of existence; and in consequence the demand for something else continued.

If we should examine closely the state of mind of the civilized world at that period, we would meet with a most interesting study, and we would realize that that period did present the psychological moment for a religion, or a higher science, that could meet the requirements of that vast number who had freed themselves from the old, but who had not found anything to take its place. We shall not take time, however, to analyze the mind of that period, nor will this be necessary, because we are all familiar with conditions as they existed at that time. We all have read much about the various movements and conditions that swayed the thought of the rising humanity fifty or sixty years ago, and, therefore, we realize what excellent soil the mentality of that period had become for the reception of the right seed. In fact, it was the very best and the very richest soil that could be desired for something that contained a vital message — something that not only aimed to possess the truth, but that could prove its claims with thorough satisfaction to all who were in need of that particular message, whatever it was to be.

It was in that soil that the seed of Christian Science was placed; and we understand fully that coming as it did at that time it found everything that could be desired for the development of a religious system of tremendous power and extraordinary proportions.

Where or how Mary Baker Eddy received her first insight into her system of thought does not matter. It is sufficient to know that she did discover a principle that has served as a solid foundation for the work of Christian Science, and will continue to serve in that manner so long as that particular movement is needed for the progress of the race. Whether she was inspired or whether she was simply endowed with an extraordinary perception of the situation so that she could understand both the requirements of the hour and the mode of supplying those requirements— this does not matter in the least, although we must admit that no one could have done what she did without being in very close contact with mental and spiritual light of a very extraordinary nature.

She took advantage of the situation in a manner that bespeaks the possession of remarkable genius along the line of her thought and undertakings; and the first stroke of genius that we find in her mode of action was in selecting the name that she did for her religion. There is indeed magic in that name. She combined the two most powerful words in the civilized world at the time, and we know these two words still are the most powerful known to the western half of the hemisphere. She did more than that. She gave a new and interior meaning, both to the word "Christian" and to the word "Science," thus doubling the spiritual power of the name she had chosen.

The word "Christianity" had been a power for nearly twenty centuries. It was a term with which all minds were familiar. It stood for something high, something wonderful, something that incorporated all the ideals, all the dreams and all the most sacred yearnings of the soul.

The term "Science" had for some time occupied a similar position, although in a different field. The scientific method had become very popular, especially in the practical world and in the educational world; and this method stood for truth positively demonstrated. All awakened minds, therefore, realized that whatever was scientific was true, and that science was in its own field a synonym for truth and demonstration. Accordingly, it was a word of remarkable power.

The founder of the Christian Science movement took those two terms, both of them the most powerful in their own realms, and combined them as the name of a new religion, a new church, a new path to emancipation; and we admit that no one but an extraordinary mind could have conceived of such an idea, or such a plan. Genius was certainly present in that mind to a remarkable degree, and we may also say that inspiration was present to a still greater degree.

In analyzing the meaning of the word "Christianity," the founder of this new religion manifested more evidence of genius and inspiration. The term "Christianity" had stood for something remarkable, but it had been associated with dark clouds, and had also been connected continually with sin, sickness, trouble, and the idea that this world is a vale of tears. The old Christian doctrine declared that it was necessary to bear these things while we remained upon earth, and that there was no way in which we might dispel the clouds. The Christian Science idea, however, took the opposite view, and literally blew the clouds away. This new religion declared that Christianity stood for freedom here and now; that salvation is not only for the future, but also for the present; and that salvation includes salvation from sickness, trouble, adversity, poverty and all the ills of life, here and now, upon this planet, in this sphere of existence.

This new interpretation brought relief to thousands and thousands, and it proved its doctrines by healing the sick, and emancipating people everywhere from all sorts of trouble, poverty, wrong, adversity, and in brief, all those conditions that had been looked upon as inevitable by the old order. This new religion went further and proved its belief by the Bible, illustrating the great fact, on every hand, that the Christ power can and should emancipate mankind here and now.

This was the message, and it was indeed a great and vital message, although others had given the same message to a certain extent for some years previously, but they had not presented that message in the same forceful manner, or under the same favorable conditions; and we know it makes all the difference in the world how truth is presented. A thousand men and women may proclaim certain new ideas to the world and still the world may not pay much attention; but when a genius appears on the scene, presenting those same ideas under the proper conditions and in the proper manner, the attention of the entire world is aroused, and we all understand the reason why. Two minds may present the same idea; with the one that idea may fall flat and produce no impression whatever, but with the other that idea may actually create a sensation. The result therefore from the coming of anything new, whether it be ordinary or extraordinary, will depend entirely upon how it is presented.

The founder of the Christian Science movement did not necessarily present something that no one had ever dreamed of before, but she did present it in a manner that was strikingly new, and under combinations and conditions that were destined to produce a sensation. In other words, she laid hold upon a marvelous idea and gave it to the world in such a way that the world could receive it and understand. It was a great stroke of genius; or we might say it was the work of exceptional inspiration. Which of the two it happened to be does not matter. It is results that we all seek, and we are not directly concerned with the definition, or the methods, or the plan.

In connection with the word "Science," the founder of this movement presented evidence of more genius. We know that that word represented facts, facts that could be demonstrated; but Mary Baker Eddy gave a new meaning to that word, and made it stand not simply for demonstration of physical facts, but also for the demonstration of truth in mind and spirit as well. She also made it stand for a certain mode of living, a mode that we have come to call constructive living, scientific living, or living and thinking according to science — science interpreted as a spiritual manifestation of truth as well as a manifestation of truth on all other planes. To be scientific, therefore, in this new science would be to establish all living and all thinking upon the principle of Divine Truth, and formulate all thought, all states of mind and all modes of living in perfect harmony with the principle of truth itself.

The idea is that Divine Truth contains within itself the principle of freedom, health, wholesomeness, power, emancipation; and therefore, in order to be scientific according to this new idea, every thought and every expression will have to give expression to that which was revealed by the understanding of the principle of truth—Absolute or Divine Truth. Herein we find the necessity of considering the word "error," which represents the sum-total of all such ideas as the mind of man may create when living in materiality, or in a state where the truth is misunderstood or not properly comprehended. To eliminate error, therefore, became one of the essentials in the emancipation of the mind from all adverse conditions that might exist either in the personality or in one's environments; and this we clearly understand because if we are to become scientific according to this new idea, we must think and express the principle of truth.

This new conception of science became a power, and for several reasons. In the first place, it was logical, that is, to those who were able to appreciate the fact that science was not necessarily confined to the physical realm, but that science stood for a principle and therefore would naturally belong in a larger measure to the spiritual realm.

In this connection we might pause and consider the criticism of those who have sometimes termed Christian Science "mere intellectual rubbish"; but no one will make that criticism unless he is confined exclusively to materiality. Anyone who is spiritually awakened, or whose mind has gained that broad conception of life where he is conscious in the spiritual as well as in the material — such a mind knows that the Christian Science interpretation of the term "science" is logical, and that it is absolutely true to the truth. We know, of course, there are a number of statements in "Science and Health" that are contradictory; but it certainly would not be possible to find any book written by human hand that would not contain some imperfections; on the whole, however, that book is a clear and lucid presentation of facts; and anyone who is trained in metaphysics, or who has the power to appreciate the metaphysical idea, can read that book from beginning to end and find it thoroughly logical, absolutely true to the truth.

This new interpretation of science also presented a new conception of life, and enlarged upon the power of science to such an extraordinary degree that anyone who might henceforth use the term science — using it in the consciousness of its new meaning — could not help but feel its wonderful power. It opened a way to the discernment of the inner side of things, the higher side, the finer side, and enabled the mind to enter into that finer spiritual conception of truth and reality that is absolutely indispensable to the understanding of real truth itself, as well as to the living of a life that may have truth and reality as its permanent foundation.

This new idea of science became powerful for another reason; and it is this, that when our thinking is scientific, that is, when we formulate thought and life in the image and likeness of our highest conception of Divine Truth, we are building up in the mind some very powerful forces — forces that are wholesome and constructive, and that invariably tend to make the whole of life a positive power for greater and greater good; and therefore anyone who lives according to science cannot fail to ascend steadily and surely into the consciousness of greater and greater good.

We know that when the mind is trained to think constructively, and think toward certain lofty ideals, and when that training is made so thorough that every element in the entire personality becomes inspired with a desire to work toward this lofty ideal — we find that the entire system begins to pass through a state of transformation; that is, both mind and body will find freedom from the lesser, from the adverse, or from the wrong, and will steadily change into the consciousness and realization of the wholesome, the true, the harmonious, and the ideal.

Herein we find the real secret of emancipation and also the real principle upon which science healing is based. It is not necessary, however, to analyze in detail the process of the scientific method, because we are all familiar with it; but we realize what an inspiration the word "science" becomes when this inner and larger meaning of science is fully understood; and it cannot fail to produce a deep and wonderful impression upon those who are prepared to understand its meaning in this higher and larger measure.

The first step, therefore, to be taken by the new movement was to combine those two wonderful words in one name, formulating thereby a religious system of thought and life that eliminated completely the dark clouds of false belief. The term "Christian" came to stand for emancipation, for health, for life, for freedom, for joy, for abundance, for the all-good of all good things, here and now; and the word "science" came to stand for a new and marvelous method, a method that could be employed and demonstrated not only in the external world, but also in the worlds of mind and spirit. We understand, therefore, that such a combination of terms and ideas, appearing at the right time, at the psychological moment, at a time when thousands were in dire need of that great message the new movement came so fully prepared to present — we fully understand why the movement became such a power, and why it has succeeded to such a remarkable degree. But back of it all was a wonderful woman, a woman who has made her place in history, a place that will be absolutely secure for all time. She has won immortal fame, and she deserves it in the fullest measure of the term.

To these facts we all agree, but what we wish to know in particular is the *real* reason why the Christian Science movement has become so powerful, and why it has succeeded to such a degree regardless of misunderstanding and opposition. We know that when we consider its origin, and the elements that went to make up the system in the beginning, we find many reasons why it necessarily would succeed; but those elements do not convey the real reason. To find the real reason we shall have to penetrate more deeply into the principles upon which the movement was based; and in this manner we shall discover something that will prove of exceptional importance to us all; that is, if we choose to apply practically and continually the secret we shall thus discover.

There are a great many things that could be mentioned if we were in search of the real reason why the Christian Science movement has been so successful, but the majority of these things would occupy a secondary position. There are two things, however, that occupy a most important position, and it is these two that are, more than all others, responsible for the success of the movement.

The first of these is the practice among Christian Scientists of living absolutely according to the metaphysical principle; and although we cannot say that their method of conforming to the metaphysical principle would constitute the highest light for everybody, still one thing is certain, and it is this, that any individual who realizes the power of Divine Truth, or that comprehends the metaphysical conception of life and who positively believes that the power of truth is sufficient to give him absolute freedom from any illness in life or bring to him anything that he may desire in life — any one who believes this, and who depends absolutely upon that understanding, is going to accomplish far more than if he relied upon that understanding part of the time, and at other times employed other or lesser means.

We have heard a great deal in modern times about the possibility of combining the different systems of cure, and whether it might be all right to take medicine and at the same time apply metaphysical treatment. The fact is, however, that it will depend largely upon the individual. There are some individuals who are not very deeply impressed by anything, but whatever means they do employ may tend to help them through good suggestions. In other words, when they take medicine they believe that this will help, and of course it does help to the extent that they accept the suggestion of helpfulness received at the time. Then they may employ science treatment and may expect help in the same way, thereby giving themselves good suggestions once more.

With these people, however, it is all suggestion, and whatever help they secure, they secure through the power of suggestion; and there are a great many people connected with the Christian Science movement who get nothing but good suggestions out of the Christian Science movement. They have not entered into the metaphysics of life in any mode or manner. They do not understand the science of the system they have adopted because they have not entered *inside,* so to speak, of the beliefs or ideas they have adopted. The only good they secure from their association with the Christian Science movement is the effect of helpful, positive and optimistic suggestions; and we know that where minds are susceptible such an influence is always beneficial, but it is also superficial and has no permanent value anywhere.

It is largely the same with a great many people who study other lines of mental or spiritual or metaphysical systems. They are benefited whenever a good suggestion is given them; but in their case it is nothing more than suggestion. The help they receive is always temporary, and they have to be helped again and again by some individual who can give them good, strong suggestions in the same way as the physician gives a dose of medicine according to requirement.

All of this, however, is on the outside, and has nothing to do with the real understanding of Divine Truth; but let any individual get into the spirit of this understanding and enter into the consciousness of real metaphysics — then he will actually gain possession of the power of truth, the power of the spirit and the power of the Christ dwelling in man; and he will find that if he continues to depend absolutely upon that power regardless of circumstances he is going to have far greater results than he could possibly have by dividing his attention among a score of different methods or systems.

The law involved therein is very simple because we understand that when we depend absolutely upon higher power and have unbounded faith in that power, the mind will constantly reach out into higher and finer realization of that power, thereby gaining possession of a greater and greater measure of that power constantly; and we understand full well that whatever the condition may be, if we gain sufficient spiritual power we will be able to eliminate adverse conditions absolutely and realize perfect freedom. On the other hand, if we have faith in higher power only now and then, and then transfer our faith to something else at frequent intervals, the house will be divided against itself. Thus we do not have real faith in anything. We are simply trying them, so to speak, to see whether they will work; but the fact is that nothing will work for us unless we first proceed with unbounded faith in the method or the principle that we have elected to employ.

We find among Christian Scientists that a great many of them are actually expressing and depending absolutely upon the power of truth. They depend exclusively upon the principle upon which they stand; that is, a fair percentage of them do, although we know that the larger percentage live undoubtedly on the outside and secure results only through superficial suggestion. This larger number have -not entered into the inner circle of truth, so to speak, and do not comprehend the spirit of truth nor the real significance of the Christian Science movement.

The real Christian Scientist, however, depends absolutely upon the power of truth, the power of the spirit, the power of the Christ — and lives, thinks and acts continually in the metaphysical state of mind, that state of mind in which the understanding of divine truth is absolutely genuine and pure.

In this connection we may ask a very important question; and the question is, if we, who do not belong to the Christian Science organization and have not adopted their system as a whole, — if we can employ the same method of depending absolutely upon the spirit and get the same results, without complying with the rules and regulations of that organization. It is a question that has been asked frequently, and there is but one answer, because we all know that the truth is not confined to any organization nor dependent upon the rules and regulations of any institution whatever. The truth is that any human soul who will depend absolutely upon the spirit of truth will receive the full power of the spirit of truth, and will secure the same results, whether he work alone or choose to unite with some institution. We must realize that we do not have to abide by any fixed system of belief or any mode of organization in order to come into the possession of the good, the true and the ideal.

It is not necessary to be loyal to this system or to that individual in order to receive spiritual power. All that is necessary is to enter into the metaphysical conception of life where we can understand truth in its purity, and thereby receive the full power of the spirit of truth; and when we do receive that power, depend absolutely upon the truth itself, never for one moment thinking that we shall have to employ something else.

The real Christian Scientists have taken this lofty position; and that is one of their great secrets. They do not compromise with the lesser under any circumstance. They take God at his word and expect him to answer every prayer here and now. We know, however, that there are not a great many people who do this. Most people pray and have faith in a measure; and then when they discover that results do not follow instantaneously, they call in a physician, or they proceed to give their attention to some other means. As a rule, they continue in this house-divided-against-itself attitude, never giving any method or process sufficient time to do its work. They are constantly scattering their forces, and therefore accomplish very little in the metaphysical or spiritual worlds.

In this connection we must not say that no one should ever call in a physician. The truth is, that if we are convinced that we are in need of a physician or that we need material help of any kind, we should seek such help at once. But the point is this: When we know that the power of the spirit can do anything for us, and when we have learned to live in a state of consciousness where we understand the truth so deeply and so perfectly that we know absolutely that the knowing of the truth can and does make for freedom invariably — if we depend absolutely upon the truth and the limitless power of the indwelling Christ, we shall find that the mere thought of seeking lesser means at any time is a waste of time. We shall gain far more and realize far greater results if we stand by the power of the truth under every circumstance, and depend so absolutely upon that power that our entire attention is directed upon the light of that understanding through which we gain possession of this power.

When we proceed to consider this phase of the subject another question may arise. We will suppose that we do depend upon the power of the spirit absolutely for a reasonable length of time; and when we do not secure results, should we then give up and try some other method? We admit this question involves a very fine point, and the answer would depend altogether upon the situation. We know that Jesus Christ did, at some times, or at any rate appeared to use material means, and used various methods at times that seemed different from the purely spiritual method. And we must admit that it is always well to consider the laws of nature in the truth as we did when we depended exclusively upon material methods. There can be no sympathy for people who purposely sit in a cold draft in order that they may be able later to demonstrate the power of science; or for people who eat anything they like in order to prove how easily they can overcome the ill effects.

The truth is, we have better use for our energy than that. Still if we realize that we are in the spirit, that we are influenced exclusively by the power of the spirit, literally filled with that power, we certainly cannot have any fear of drafts or anything else. Nevertheless, there is no need of subjecting the body to extra work under any circumstance. This entire field involves many fine points, and we shall have to judge for ourselves what we are going to do under these circumstances. At the present time we all have physical bodies, and we are surrounded with many conditions that are imperfect or adverse, so that we shall find it advisable to exercise all the wisdom we possess in order to adapt ourselves harmoniously to everything that may arise in this sphere of existence.

THE GOOD SIDE OF CHRISTIAN SCIENCE 19

But regardless of this we know that the principal secret of the Christian Science movement is found in this: That they depend absolutely upon the power of the truth and the power of the indwelling Christ. They have taken God at his word, and expect him to answer every prayer without the least doubt. They believe that in the spirit and in the truth there is health and freedom for everybody; they expect to demonstrate health and freedom by living absolutely and continuously in the spirit of truth; and they have results, wonderful results. What they have accomplished is an illustration of what can be accomplished by devoted and consecrated concentration upon higher spiritual power. It is an illustration of what can be done when we follow the great statement, "Keep the eye single upon the Most High"; and those who understand the psychology of this process will realize at once why the Christian Science movement has accomplished so much and become such a marvelous power in the religious world today.

It is not necessary to analyze this phase of the subject further, because we know that people are coming more and more to the conclusion that after we have entered into the understanding of the greater, and after we have come to a place where we really know what higher power can do, it is certainly a waste of time to give any attention whatever to the lesser. And we are also coming more and more into the realization of the truth that the more devoted we are to the power of the spirit, and the more perfectly we live in the pure metaphysical understanding of Divine Truth, the greater will the power of the spirit manifest in us and through us. This is a principle we all understand; but it is something that we should not simply remember; it is something that deserves our deepest and most thorough attention.

Another principle of practice that has proven so highly important in the success of the Christian Science movement is that of giving absolute devotion to the great central idea of the system itself. The term "Christian Science" stands for a certain idea. That idea may be vague to some minds, but to those who really understand it, or who have looked into it carefully, it becomes an idea that represents something that is not only definite but something of marvelous meaning.

On every hand we hear people making the statement when in dangerous places, "Suppose we try science." That word has come to mean something special; and even the outside world is beginning to appreciate the fact that there is power back of the term "Science," although they may not understand where or how that power produces results.

The majority, however, among those who have gained some understanding of the principle of real science, believe firmly that the power existing or manifesting through science has the power to protect, to heal, to emancipate and to bring us every good thing in life. In other words, science, with its interior interpretation, represents a power that can make all things right here and now; and those who have entered into this interior interpretation actually feel that they are protected by something that is invincible, something that comes from a higher and unlimited source.

We find that Christian Scientists, as a rule, realize that the central idea of the system they have adopted contains a superior power, or is the channel through which superior power can be realized; and by concentrating attention upon that idea they enter more and more into the realization of the power itself, thereby securing all the protection, all the guidance and all the benefit that their understanding of the idea can produce for them as far as they have gone in their understanding at the present time.

There are quite a number, however, among the more devoted Christian Scientists that have concentrated their attention so exclusively upon this central idea that they have become fanatical, and therefore are becoming in a measure an obstacle to their own higher achievement. That, however, is another story, and is something that we need not enter into at the present time.

The principle is this, that whenever you have an ideal of enormous possibilities, and devote yourself absolutely to that ideal, that is, concentrate your whole life upon everything that is high, wonderful or marvelous in that ideal — then you not only place in action all the greater powers within yourself, but you also place yourself in a position where you are constantly reaching out and up into the higher and better understanding of all the powers and possibilities that do exist in that ideal. The result is that you will enter more and more into the inheritance of that ideal; and where that ideal involves the absolute understanding of Divine Truth you will enter more and more into the spirit of that truth, thereby fulfilling in your own life that wonderful statement, "Ye shall know the Truth, and the Truth shall make you free."

To state it differently, if you know of a certain power that can do certain things, and you devote yourself absolutely to that power all through your life, there is only one conclusion to come to, and it is this, that one of these days that power is going to return your favor. You will enter into the possession of that power, and all that is beautiful and marvelous in that power will become your own.

The Christian Scientists are proving this every day. They are devoting themselves absolutely to the great central principle of Divine Truth, and have consecrated themselves in every form and manner to the invincible power of Divine Truth. The result is that that power is returning the favor; and therefore they are proving their religion in every form and manner.

In this connection, however, we must remember that the secret of the Christian Scientist will not be found in the belief that they know more than other people, although they certainly do know more than a great many people; but their secret is found in their tremendous devotion to a high spiritual idea and a high spiritual power. They do not comprehend the mysteries of life any more perfectly than other devoted students of the same subject, but they have entered into the metaphysical conception of truth; and this has given them the key to the real understanding of truth and the real power of the spirit. But this key is not the sole possession of the Christian Scientist, nor will it become, at any time, the sole possession of any one organization.

The truth is that any individual who will enter into the metaphysical conception of truth and devote his life absolutely and exclusively to the spirit of the truth as discerned in the consciousness of pure metaphysics — let any individual take this same course, and he will also find the same key.

It is an illustration of tremendous concentration or consecration of the highest order. We know that concentration is the great key to achievement in all modes of demonstration; but we cannot apply the principle of concentration unless we have something upon which to concentrate that really does contain the power that we desire. And here we must also remember that concentration does not express its greatest power until it becomes consecration; that is, the attitude of mind must become metaphysical and spiritual, and must devote itself absolutely to the highest truth and the inner or spiritual significance of absolute truth.

We all will admit that one of the greatest lessons to be learned at the present time is this lesson of unprecedented spiritual concentration or consecration of Divine Truth as manifested in the Christian Science movement; and we all may say to ourselves, and wisely, "Go, and do likewise"; although we need not unite with that movement in order to demonstrate the same truth and the same power.

The Christian Science system is a system that is admirably adapted to a large number of people, but the way it is organized at the present time is not adapted to everybody; and when no organization or system of belief can possess the exclusive secret to the perfect understanding of truth, we realize that we may employ this same principle no matter where we may live or work, or through what system of belief we may prefer to express ourselves in this age.

When we study this wonderful subject, we find that certain interpretations of truth become, so to speak, channels or pathways toward that higher understanding or consciousness that we are in search of; and although there may be any number of such interpretations, complying with the various needs of various people, they all may lead to the same

THE GOOD SIDE OF CHRISTIAN SCIENCE

sublime source. Our first object therefore should be to learn the understanding of the great law, that law of life that we all must employ in our search for the realization of the whole truth concerning life; and whenever we do employ that law we will enter into the very truth that we desire, that we have searched for. And whenever we are in the truth, we know the truth, and accordingly gain the absolute freedom promised.

In this connection we should also remember the fact that it is not what we believe, or what institutions we belong to, or what systems we have adopted — it is not these things that bring results; it is *what we do with the principle involved* — that is what brings results.

In considering this subject further, we might ask another question; that is, how it happened that the Christian Science movement almost from the beginning entered into this wonderful secret — the application of the wonderful law of spiritual concentration or consecration; and we also might ask why they succeeded in finding the inner or metaphysical conception of truth and life — the consciousness of the purely metaphysical state, thought and being.

In answer, we know that there were various reasons. One reason was the way the movement began; and these two wonderful words, "Christian" and "Science," were so combined that their interior meaning made a powerful impression upon those people who were ready to appreciate that interior meaning, and who entered into that attitude of mind where their consciousness of the spiritual side became a reality.

And here let us consider a remarkable psychological law. Whenever you find the inner meaning of any principle, law or state of being, and are in a position to be deeply impressed by the inner meaning thus discerned, and furthermore consecrate attention with mind and soul and spirit upon this inner meaning, you will soon enter into the real consciousness of that interior state.

You will find thereby that you have discovered a new world in the domains of mind and spirit, a world in which you may remain all your life if you continue to be true to the highest truth that you have discerned within that world.

The early Christian Scientists discerned the inner meaning of Christian Science; that is, the interior meaning of the central idea or principle that was represented by the Christian Science system. They were ready for it, inasmuch as they had outgrown literalism absolutely; and being ready for it — hungering and thirsting for the consciousness of the spirit, they absolutely consecrated mind and soul and spirit upon the great Light that had been revealed to them.

Accordingly, they entered into the very life and spirit of that Light; and they found after they had passed through the "inner gates" that they were in an attitude of mind they had never known before. This attitude of mind we know to be the attitude of pure metaphysics; that is, an attitude that transcends all conditions and things — an attitude that involves an absolute consciousness of the reality of eternal being.

They discovered that while in that attitude, usually termed "the spiritual understanding of Divine Truth," they were able to demonstrate the power of truth; and whenever we can demonstrate the power of truth we have an argument in favor of our position that is invincible.

The Christian Science method, therefore, of finding the interior significance and power of real truth was a method that demonstrated itself admirably. And here we may emphasize the fact that, as far as we know, the meaning of Christianity and the inner meaning of Science had never been combined before into one great spiritual idea; and therefore those who were ready, hungering and thirsting for the spiritual, would naturally enter into this new understanding with unbounded enthusiasm and limitless faith.

It would be possible, if we should so desire, to illustrate this process along psychological lines, and demonstrate all the laws involved, explaining every step made in a thoroughly scientific manner; but those of us who have more or less discernment of the inner meaning of all great principles, can discern at once why the Christian Science movement gained at the very beginning a position that was indeed founded on the solid rock.

The methods employed were methods based upon the great law of spiritual understanding; and they have produced remarkable results; but they are not the only methods, because the spiritual world is wonderfully rich.

We may expect, therefore, that almost at any time in the future another method for approaching Divine Truth may be evolved, and another system of thought with another institution appearing to further that method throughout the world — an institution that may become far greater and far more powerful than the Christian Science movement is today.

The fact that there are ten times as many people outside the Christian Science Church as inside that church who are searching for the highest truth, not being satisfied with the Christian Science method, proves conclusively that there is an overwhelming demand for some other means or process through which the marvelous power of the spirit may be gained and demonstrated here and now; and we know that wherever the demand is sufficiently large, the supply must follow in due time.

The Christian Science movement has filled the spiritual wants, as well as the temporal wants of thousands and thousands of people; but that movement is not able to supply the spiritual or temporal wants of all the people who have awakened to the new light, the new time and the new order.

We realize therefore that if the law of demand and supply is to be true, and it always is true, the time is ripe for another spiritual movement, a movement that will far transcend the Christian Science movement, both in spirituality and in power.

When that movement shall arise no one can say at the present time; but there is one thing we should remember in our study of this great subject; and it is this, that whenever a group of people unite in harmony upon a certain idea, or a certain lofty goal, or a certain sublime principle, and proceed to work together with unbounded devotion for the realization of that principle, the power contained within that principle will, sooner or later, return the favor and bring those people the very thing they want.

We must remember the great law that whenever we find an ideal, or a wonderful spiritual light containing within itself remarkable powers and possibilities, and when we devote ourselves absolutely to that light, having unlimited faith in its power, the time will come, and come shortly, when the truth and the power of that light will begin to manifest in us; that is, the truth and the power of that light will begin to express itself in all our thought and action and enable us more and more to demonstrate the law according to our highest ideals and our most perfect faith.

There are a great many things that could be added to this study, but we are interested principally in the fundamental or inner secret of results everywhere. If any man or any institution is gaining ground we wish to know why; but we do not want to feel that we have to adopt the system of any particular individual or institution, or do what he is doing in exactly the same mode or manner, because we all are individuals, and will have to express our individuality more and more if we are to advance in the scale of life.

But if any particular individual has an inner secret, we wish to learn and understand that secret. We wish to understand the reason why he is securing results.

We wish to understand the psychological side everywhere, because we know that if the psychological side is studied carefully we shall learn exactly how these higher laws operate, why they succeed at certain times, or through certain people, and why they fail at other times.

We know there are many things that will have to be considered in connection with any movement or principle that has achieved wonderfully; but the principal thing involved is this, that unlimited devotion to some sublime idea, some idea that stands for something remarkable, an idea that has a vital message, or an idea that contains the power to do things along new and wonderful lines — unlimited devotion to such an idea will invariably bring wonderful results; and the more perfectly we can enter into the metaphysical attitude as we proceed, thereby laying hold of the real understanding or principle itself, the greater will be the results we have in view.

Herewith we might inquire more thoroughly into the nature of the metaphysical attitude with a view of learning exactly why results invariably increase when we proceed through that attitude; but we appreciate the fact that this would involve a very large study, although it is a study that we must by no means ignore in the future.

The majority of us, however, have had so much experience along this line that we can see at once the inner meaning of that phase of the subject. And here we may well repeat that any person, or any system, or any institution that has found this higher or inner meaning, and that is making full and effective application of the principle involved, must certainly receive our highest admiration.

In the first place, we cannot help giving our admiration to any individual or institution that is demonstrating the law in a wonderful manner; and, in the second place, we shall find it most profitable to admire and respect every individual or institution that is demonstrating in this manner; for the fact is that whenever we admire or appreciate the greater, we enter into the spirit of the greater, and therefore establish in our own lives an upward and onward tendency.

We affirm that each individual should do his best work under every circumstance, employing what method he may think best; and we do demand that every individual or institution do the very best that he can with the method that he has adopted. But the question is, if there are very many individuals or institutions that are really doing their best with what they have. And inasmuch as the Christian Science movement is certainly doing its very best with the principle and system it has adopted as its own, that movement deserves the highest admiration that can possibly be given by any and every human soul.

True, there are other institutions that are just as devoted to their ideals and that are also trying to make full and effective application of the principles upon which they stand.

To these we must also give our highest admiration, because they are all moving in the same direction, toward the same great goal, approaching the same great Light. And while we are moving upward and onward in this wonderful manner we want to realize the highest and greatest possibilities along our own lines of action, and not waste energy criticising other individuals or institutions that may be using methods slightly different from our own.

This is certainly good sound doctrine, and it has deep psychological significance. We all should apply it therefore; and above all we should remember the one great principle once more, that whenever you discover any system of truth, or any great idea, or any wonderful power — then consecrate yourself absolutely to that idea or power, devoting yourself to the greatest and the highest that you can possibly discern in the life of that idea or power, and the result will be that that power will return the favor and do for you what you expected, or according to your faith; and inasmuch as spiritual power is limitless, there is nothing that that power cannot do.

If we fail in its use, the fault is ours; we have not devoted ourselves absolutely to our highest understanding of spiritual power. We may have scattered our forces or worshiped too many lesser gods.

Henceforth, however, let us worship the highest that we know, and worship absolutely by keeping the eye singly upon the great light and the one great power, inspiring our worship with a passion for the sublime — a passion so strong and so deep that it stirs every atom of the soul. The results will be exactly what we have expected; our prayers will be answered; our ideals will be made real; and everything that we have wanted or desired in life shall come to us according to our faith.

THE END

www.ingramcontent.com/pod-product-compliance
Lightning Source LLC
LaVergne TN
LVHW092102060526
838201LV00047B/1534